THE DOCTRINE OF THE LAST THINGS

THE DOCTRINE OF THE LAST THINGS

OBADIAH E. HARRIS

J Merrill Publishing, Inc.
434 Hillpine Drive
Columbus, OH 43207
www.JMerrill.pub

Library of Congress Control Number: 9781954414440
ISBN-13: 978-1-954414-44-0 (Paperback)
ISBN-13: 978-1-954414-43-3 (eBook)

Book Title: The Doctrine of the Last Things
Author: Obadiah E. Harris
Cover Design: Terri L. Bea-Sopher

For my Family

CONTENTS

FOREWARD

Pastor Obadiah E. Harris, Sr., is also the author of the Amazon Best Seller "The Celestial Advantage." He is the Senior Pastor of Lifting Up Jesus Church in Chillicothe, Ohio. He is the husband of Karen A. Harris. The father of Obadiah

(Andrea) and Karrin. The grandfather of Donavin Baker, Eldrick, Obadiah "Jesiah," and Henry Harris.

I dedicate this work to my deceased parents Obadiah Harris Jr. & Evangelist, Mary Ellen Harris, and my deceased brother Bernard they continue to inspire my desire! I also want to thank my brother Bishop Tim Harris for his support as we endure in the Jesus-Harris mission!

"Then Peter said unto them, Repent, and be baptized every one of you in the name of Jesus Christ for the remission of sins, and ye shall receive the gift of the Holy Ghost."

— ACTS 2:38 KJV

1

ESCHATOLOGY

The Biblical account explicitly defines God's singular authorship of man, the world, and all of creation. The Genesis creation account states unequivocally that in the beginning, God created. Yet, the term Genesis is associated with such English words as generic, generation, and generate.

To generate means to get something started, which undoubtedly constitutes God's role as the ignition developer behind all things.

In Hebrews 12, Christ Jesus is appropriately referred to as the author and finisher of our faith. The term author is the Greek word "ARCHEGOS," which signifies one who takes a lead in or provides the first occasion of anything. An "ARCHEGOS" can be the head of a family, a pioneer blazing a path for futuristic travelers, or one who takes precedence in faith and is thus the perfect example of it.

To define Christ or God in terms of authorship only would be an injustice to the scope of God's continuing activity. God's prominence is established by what He has done, is doing, and will do.

Hebrews 12 also defines Christ as being the finisher of our faith. The Greek word for finisher is "TELEIOTES," which translates as perfecter or one who brings something to completion.

The book of Revelation presents Christ as the "ALPHA" and the "OMEGA."

The term "ALPHA" and "OMEGA" describe the Greek alphabet's first and the last letters, or accommodated to our English linguistics from A to Z.

The term "ESCHATOLOGY" is the offspring of the Greek word "ESCHATOS," which means "LAST" and "LOGOS," also meaning "SUBJECT OR ORDERED STATEMENT." ESCHATOLOGY, therefore, deals with the "TELEIOTES," or the completion phases of God's earthly program: The "OMEGA" or "Z" era of God's alphabetical prophetical consummation. In laymens' terms, "ESCHATOLOGY" deals with the doctrine of the last things. Thus, events such as the Rapture of the Church, the Tribulation period, the Second Coming of Christ, the Millennium." and the New Heaven, and the New Earth all fall within the "ESCHATOLOGY" categorization of climactic events.

In dealing with prophetic predictions, both the prophet's credibility and the accuracy of the prophecies are meticulously scrutinized. But beyond any shadow of a doubt, both Christ and the Bible have passed the tests of human criticality with flying colors.

In the science of Geology, its scholars speak of the earth being in a state called "ISOSTASY" as the earth rotates on its orbital revolutions. The law of "Isostasy" says that there must be an Equal balance of landmass and water mass for the earth to remain stable as it rotates. A discovery of this magnitude invites temptation to acknowledge man's ingenuity until we read the Biblical account. In Isaiah 40:12, Isaiah inspirationally wrote that God "MEASURED THE WATERS IN THE HOLLOW OF HIS HAND" and meted out heaven with the span, and comprehended the dust of the earth in a measure, and that "HE WEIGHED THE MOUNTAINS ON THE SCALES AND THE HILLS IN BALANCES."

Therefore God is revealed as the author of the earth's geological balance stabilization system. ,

In Eschatology, God's omniscience is equally evident and obvious as God declares what will happen before it happens. Jesus prophesied in Matthew 24 concerning the prevailing characteristics of the signs of His coming and the end of the world. With his telescopic vision, He saw in advance the present chaotic conditions, the earthquakes, the wars and rumors of wars, nations rising against nations, false messiahs, the refrigeration of love, etc. Though He prophesied concerning the pandemic proliferation of evil, He made it crystal clear that He's coming to deliver His people.

The Eschatology study reveals "that the earth is the Lord's and the fullness thereof, the world and they that dwelleth therein. As we scan, peruse, and investigate, it is indisputably apparent that God saves His best for last.

2

THE RAPTURE

In Genesis chapter 2, the original God-ordained union of Adam and Eve is recorded. Despite Adam's supremacy over the animals, Adam had no helpmate for fellowship, companionship, or humanity's race propagation purposes. Therefore God caused a deep sleep to come upon Adam, utilized His surgical skills removing one of Adam's ribs, and used the rib to make the woman.

In Ephesians 5, the Apostle Paul elaborated on the marital institution and, in climaxing his exposition, stated, "this is a great mystery, but I speak concerning Christ and the Church.

The correlation between Adam and Eve and Christ and the Church is very apparent. In Christ's substitutionary sacrifice for humanity, He passed into a deep sleep called death He was pierced in His side. As a result, His elect lady, the Church, was formed.

Christ's love for His Church was supremely incomparable and devoting. But he had to return to glory after His death, burial, and resurrection.

In understanding His redemptive purpose and His divine mission, Christ prepared the disciples for His ultimate departure.

In John 14, Christ encouraged His disciples to "let not your heart be troubled." He declared that His purpose in departing was, "I go to prepare a place for you, but I will come again. In this passage, He declared that in His Father's House were "many mansions." The phrase "many. mansions" actually may mean "dwelling places." This presentation of Jesus may refer to the Israelite custom of families living together in close association.

As his sons successively married, the Israelite father would add an extra room for each additional family. Eventually, the original dwelling would become a set of dwellings that enclosed a patio in the middle.

Jesus promised a heavenly residence to His disciples, not down the street from the father, but in the Father's House. Such an illustration would certainly cause visions of eternal adjacency or close relational proximity between God and His people. So instead, the bride was lovingly brought into the Father's house, which was expanded because of her.

Though Christ returned to Heaven after accomplishing His redemptive purpose, He did not leave His people comfortless (GR. "ORPHANOS") or as orphaned children.

Christ had promised His disciples another "COMFORTER," the Holy Ghost, to internalize them with power from on High. Ephesians 1:13-14 reveals the inestimable privilege available to the household of faith. The fact that true believers become the glorious recipients of the Holy Ghost of promise, which is the earnestness of our inheritance.

The term "Earnest" is from the Greek word "ARRABON," which means "ENGAGEMENT RING."

Among the Jews, the betrothal or engagement process was much more serious and permanent than the westernized culture.

The engagement often lasted a year and served as a time of probation and testing of fidelity.

The passage reveals that for 2,000 years, the Church has been the expectant bride of Christ. He has given His engagement pledge, the Holy Ghost, as insurance of this marriage's imminent and ultimate consummation, ordained in Heaven. The Bible says we have "this treasure in earthen vessels." Oh, what an expensive ring for Christ's elect lady.

The term "RAPTURE" evokes images of emotional and spiritual ecstasy. But from a Biblical perspective, it refers to an event that unites Christ, the prospective Bridegroom, with the Church, the prospective bride.

While the term RAPTURE" is a Biblical idea, it is not a Biblical term.

"RAPTURE" is derived from the Latin Vulgate Bible's usage of the word "RAPERE," which means to be "caught up."

The Apostle Paul in I Thessalonians 4:16-18 refers to this grand event. For the Lord himself shall descend from heaven with a shout, with the voice of the archangel, and with the trump of God: and the dead in Christ shall rise first: Then we which are alive and remain shall be caught up together with them in the clouds, to meet the Lord in the air: and so shall we ever be with the Lord.

The magnitude of this event is indisputably evident in the fact that "Christ Himself" descends from Heaven. Though reigning for 2,000 years with sovereignty over the world, no other event has occasioned His physical and visible appearance. · But in doctrinal consistency with the parable of the ten virgins in Matthew 25, the Bridegroom (Christ) comes for His bride.

The Thessalonians' account states the Lord Himself will descend with "a shout." The term shout is a Greek word that means a call, a summons, a shout of command, or command. The passage reveals the authoritative nature of Christ's shout of command, as two categorizations of believers are "CAUGHT UP" to meet the Lord in the air.

The Lord demonstrates His omnipotence as He defies the laws of gravity and causes in sequential order first, the dead "IN CHRIST" to be "CAUGHT UP" and then the alive believers to be caught up also. I Thessalonians 5:23 term "coming" of our Lord is the Greek word "PAROUSIA," which means "Presence or Arrival." It was used in Hellenistic Greek to designate the visit of a ruler. So indeed "THE RULER," the King of Kings, and Lord of Lords' graces the atmosphere with Divine visitation.

Paul also states that the sound of a "TRUMP will accompany this time of celebratory ecstasy." The mention of a "TRUMP" evokes memories of ancient Israel. Israel yearly commemorated a feast called the Feast of Trumpets. Today the Jews call this feast "ROSH HASHANAH," the Head of the Months, and celebrate it as the beginning of the new year. They send new year's greetings on this day, though Exodus 12 establishes the Passover as the first month of the year.

A Jew living in the Jerusalem area would have his ears keenly tuned for the sound of the trumpet during this festival season.

The moment the Jewish worshipper would hear the trumpet blast, he would cease his harvesting activities. A Jew and a foreigner may have been working side by side, but the Jew would instantly depart when the trumpet sounded, but the Gentile would keep working.

Jesus, in Matthew 24, spoke of His coming in such terms of separation. In verses 40-42, He stated, "then two shall be in the field, the one shall be taken and the other left."

Two women shall be grinding at the mill: the one shall be taken and the other left. He (Jesus) states soberly, "watch therefore: for ye know not what hour your Lord doth come."

In verse 43, to illustrate the clandestine nature of the Rapture, He compares this event "to a thief," who would break into a house at the least expected time.

In I Corinthians 15, the Apostle Paul provides further enlightenment on the subject matter of the Rapture.

He teaches that this event is somewhat incomprehensible to the unbelievers who live outside of Christ's Divine disclosures. In verse 51 expounding on the Rapture, Paul states, "Behold I shew you a mystery." The term mystery is a derivative of the Greek word "MUSTERION," a phrase associated in the Greco-Roman usage as a secret known only to initiated members. The mystery religions of antiquities were secret, exclusive groups based upon secret oaths, rites, laws, and books. To gain admittance to the location lodge of the membership, one had to know the password.

To the Christians, his entrance into the mental and spiritual comprehension of the Rapture is exclusively his. The new birth salvation experience has catapulted him into Christ's family. For he has discovered the "password," Jesus Christ, which opens the door of secrets to all of God's Divine realities.

Paul also elaborates in this 51st verse concerning the transformation that will take place in the bodily constitution of the raptured masses. He states concerning this mystery, "we shall not all sleep (die), but we shall all be changed. The change introduced in this passage corresponds to the corroborative scripture in Philippians 3, which reveals that Christ "shall change our vile body, that it may be fashioned like unto His glorious body." The term "shall change" is originated from the Greek word "METASCHEMATIZO" which means to change in fashion or appearance. The term is associated with our English word "METAMORPHOSE" or "METAMORPHOSIS." Christ is revealed as the one who shall cause a "METAMORPHOSIS," a process that changes a caterpillar, a wormlike insect of repulsion and ugliness into a butterfly, an object of stylistic design and artistic beauty. Such a pictorial illustration of transformation, from a hairy crawling insect to a high flying multi-colored adorable butterfly, certainly elevates the estimate of the transformation Rapture body.

The resurrected or glorified body majestically produced at the Rapture certainly will be a source of awe as we discover the limitless inherent potential of the celestial body. In John, the 20th chapter, as the disciples of Jesus were assembled, being intimidated because of the Jewish threat of killing them, as Christ was killed. This passage reports in verse 19 that when the doors were shut where the disciples were, Jesus came and stood in the midst.

Certainly, the disciples were amazed beyond explanation as Jesus entered the room of their assembly without the shut door being opened.

Jesus, in His resurrection body, possessed the capacity of changing from a visible to the invisible bodily constitution and therefore was able to walk through a closed door as if it were an open door. St. Luke 24 records another incident in which Christ displayed this same power of invisibility in His resurrected body as verse 31 reports. He vanished out of their sight.

Paul in I Corinthians 15:39-40 detailed God's flesh diversification in manufacturing His multiple creatures.

God uniquely created each order of beings, men, beasts, fishes, and birds, to effectively dwell in their own environmental habitat. Therefore Paul presents the glory of the Raptured saints' resurrected bodies, which will possess the constitutional capacity of functional adaptability in the celestial or heavenly sphere.

The Apostle in I Corinthians 15:52 inspirationally and impressionistically presents the Rapture's imminency and instantaneous nature.

He declares that this great event will occur in "a moment in the twinkling of an eye.

The term "moment" is from the word "ATOMOS," from which our modern scientific word "ATOM" is derived. "ATOMOS" denotes that which is indivisible or cannot be divided or cut. Therefore time in its most extreme minute quantity will be Divinely utilized to expedite the First Resurrection and the Rapture dynamics.

Paul doubles his statement of the Rapture's instantaneous occurrence by stating that it will occur in the "twinkling of an eye. The term twinkling presents another vision of the accelerated, rapid development of the Rapture. The etymon "RHIPE," which is akin to "RHIPTO," meaning "to hurl," is employed.

The term was used for any rapid movements, such as the hurling of a javelin or the rushing of wind. The inference is that the event will happen so rapidly that Christ will come before we can blink an eye, and without being noticed, the Church will be gone.

With great dispensational insight, the Apostle John describes the climactic features of the Church age. In Revelation chapter 2:1, Christ walks in the midst of the Church occupying or being the central figure.

In Revelation 2–3, John wrote to the seven churches of Asia, distinguishing the favorable and unfavorable prevailing attributes of each Church. The presentation revealed a totality of characteristics and a composite view of every type of Church and member.

Then after this Divine message,   in Revelation chapter 4, John looks, and a door was opened in Heaven. He states that the first voice I heard was like a trumpet talking with me, which said, come up hither.

The mention of the trumpet at the climax of the Church discourse and the command to "come up hither" to Heaven, along with the Church's disappearance from the earthly discussion, certainly indicates the expiration of the Church age. The Church is no more in view until Revelation chapter 19, during the Marriage Supper of the Lamb.

It is important to comprehend that the believers resurrected at the Rapture constitute the first segment of the First Resurrection. The Scripture states, "Blessed and holy is he that has a part in the first Resurrection.

It is also essential to understand that the second segment of the First Resurrection, resurrecting the Tribulation Saints, will occur before the 1,000-year reign of Christ. As corroborated by Revelation 11:4-5, John saw this persevering multitude and stated that "they lived and reigned with Christ a thousand years. But the rest of the dead lived not again until the thousand years were finished. This is the "First Resurrection."

3

THE JUDGMENT OF THE BELIEVERS' WORKS

With the Church safely transported to Heaven and reveling in the splendor of their deliverance from the earthly proving or testing ground. The book of Revelation Chapter 4 records a time of commendation, a Heavenly awards ceremony of the most exalted magnitude.

The Apostle John, in his living realization of the Rapture preview, was Divinely commanded to "Come up hither, and I will shew thee things which must be hereafter.

The immediate figure encountered in the passage is God almighty. He is enthroned in His incomparable omnipotence.

Around the throne of God are four and twenty elders sitting and clothed in white raiment and honored with gold crowns on their heads. The honored group is the obvious recipient of spiritual rewards after God's judgment of their works.

The issue of judgment is a subject expansively elaborated on in the Biblical account.

The Judgment of sin, the Judgment of the Jews in the Tribulation period, the Judgment of Nations, the Great White Throne of Judgment, but here the subject of exploration is the Judgment of the Believers Works.

The Bible states, in II Corinthians 5:10, "For we must all appear before the judgment seat of Christ, that everyone may receive the things done in his body, according to what he hath done, whether good or bad."

The issue at this judgment is not condemnation, damnation, or punishment. So obviously, if the believers make it in the Rapture, their salvation is already a Divinely eternally settled issue.

The Bible declares God's judicial omniscience through the operation of His Word in Hebrews 4:12. The passage states that "the word of God... is a discerner of the thoughts and intents of the heart."

The term "DISCERNER" originates from the word "KRITIKOS," which gives birth to the English words criticize, critique, and criticality. The passage reveals God's positive ascertainment of man's hidden meanings and motives. Therefore God possesses the judicial objectivity and the infallible impartiality to see not only what man does but why man does what he does.

In I Corinthians the third chapter, the Apostle Paul expounds on the details of the Judgment of Works.

In verse 10, he refers to himself as a "wise master builder." He exhorts the Church regarding the necessary prerequisite of being foundationally established upon Christ.

In verses 11-12, Paul introduces two different categories of works. Each will be tested by fire to determine what sort it is.

He states that the believers' works, when tested by fire, either has combustibility or non-combustibility.

The works Divinely determined to be qualitatively similar to wood, hay, and stubble cause the believer "to suffer loss, but he himself shall be saved."

When tried by fire, the qualitative category of gold, silver, and precious stones prove their Divine acceptance by enduring the fire test. The testing of fire is within the judgmental determinations of Christ. Revelations 1:14 reveals Christ as possessing eyes that were as a flame of fire.

The New Testament records five different crowns available to the triumphant Christian.

1. The "Crown of Life" in Jas. 1:12 and Revelation 2:10.
2. The "Crown of Glory in I Peter 5:2-4.
3. The "Crown of Rejoicing" in I Thess, 2:19-20.
4. The "Crown of Righteousness" in II Timothy 4-8.
5. The "Incorruptible Crown" in I Corinthians 9:25-7.

The 24 elders in the Revelation chapter 4 passage and verse 4 are clothed in white raiment. They are the obvious recipients of the promise in Revelation 3:4 that he that overcometh shall walk with me in white for they are worthy.

The 24 elders are wearing "Crowns of gold (STEPHANOS). They are "sitting," denoting the fact that they are now resting in the heavenly places. It is believed that the 24 represents the totality of redeemed believers of both the old and the New Testament.

When the games were over in the ancient Grecian contestations, the runners, wrestlers, and successful contestants assembled before the "Bema or Judges stand," an elevated seat where the umpire sat the winner received a "corruptible crown" or laurel leaves. Some had no reward, for they had lost the "Victor's Crown   ." However, there was no reward,   no punishment, and they were not cast out, which is an apparent cultural allusion to the judgment of works by fire in I Cor. 4.

But in this Revelation 4 passage, the overcomers receive the "STE-PHANOS" Crown of commendation. A Crown designated for the "Victors." The saints raptured and being illustrated through the 24 elders were assembled before the eternal Judgment Seat, "BEMA," and received their "CROWNS" from God for keeping the faith.

But in demonstrated humility, in Revelation 4:10-11, the 24 Elders fell down. They recognized the superlative privilege of being in the presence of

The Lord. "Thou art worthy, O Lord, to receive Glory and Honor, and Power: for Thou hast created all things, and for thy pleasure, they are and were created. Yes, in bowing down, they recognized the one and only King of Kings and threw down their crowns because He alone is worthy!

4

THE TRIBULATION PERIOD

The vast masses of Christianity are radically divided over the Tribulation Period issue.

The terminology "Tribulation Period" refers to an Eschatological period of unprecedented persecution, torture, and death that will last for seven years under the domination of the Antichrist.

It is a period mysteriously designed by God for Israel, particularly for the unregenerate secondarily and indirectly.

Jeremiah 30:4-7 calls it a time of "Jacob's Trouble," an obvious allusion to Israel in the Old Testament. In: Ezekiel 20:34-38, this period is called a time when Israel shall "pass under the rod" or experience Divine chastening.

Ezekiel 22:19-22 God presents Himself as a specialist in the field of metallurgy. First, God presents Jerusalem as His melting pot or the place of His providential purifying of Israel. God then forecasts His purposeful engagement of applying heat (Tribulation) to Israel to refine her like gold.

In the middle or at the three and one half year segment of this period, expressions of violence reach their all-time high. Daniel 12:1 gives a prophetical synopsis of this period as a time of trouble that never existed since there was a nation. Jesus seconds the motion of Daniel's assessment by saying, in Matthew 24:21, concerning the later three and one half year period that it will be characterized "by great tribulation, such as has not occurred since the beginning of the world."

Highly opinionated Tribulation advocates vary in that some are proponents of the Pre-Tribulation doctrine, others Mid-Tribulation, some Post Tribulation, and some believe in no Tribulation at all.

The Pre-Tribulation doctrine states that the Church will be raptured before the Tribulation

Period.

The Mid-Tribulation doctrine states that the Rapture will occur in the middle of the Tribulation period.

The Post-Tribulation doctrine states that the Rapture will occur after the Tribulation period.

The Biblical position or doctrinal stance on the Tribulation period is Pre-Tribulation.

Jesus, in His teachings, presented two different periods as possessing moral and spiritual characteristics parallel to those prior to His coming. The days of Noah before the Flood and the days of Lot before the incineration of Sodom and Gomorrah.

In Matthew 24:37, Jesus states, "but as the days of Noah were, so shall also the coming of the "Son of Man be."

Jesus then, in verse 38, enumerates the degenerate character prevalent in the antediluvian era as being one of excess of indulgences, debauchery, polygamy, and spiritual nonchalance. They "were eating, drinking, marrying, and giving in marriage until the day that Noah entered into the ark." And knew not until the Flood came and took them all away so shall also the coming of the Son of Man be.

In Luke 17:28-30, Jesus reveals the striking similarity existing between Lot's age and this present age IN the days of Lot; they did eat, they drank, they bought, they sold, they planted, they builded. But, the same day that Lot went out of Sodom, it rained fire and brimstone from heaven and destroyed them all. Even thus shall it be in the day when the Son of Man is revealed.

Truly no treatment of the Rapture, the Tribulation period, or Eschatology would be complete without an inspection of God's typical dealings with Noah and his family. The great event of the Flood must not be incorrectly viewed as an event with no prior Divine warning or opportunity for radical moral and spiritual rectification.

Noah preached for 120 years (Genesis 6:3) concerning the coming Flood. The knowledge of the coming Judgment was first revealed to his father Lamech, through his father Methuselah, and through Methuselah's father, Enoch.

In viewing this era, we can see the typical representation of the Biblically defined classifications of people, as corroborated by I

Corinthians 10:32, Jews, Gentiles, and the Church of God.

Enoch, Noah's great grandfather, is one of two Old Testament saints along with Elijah, who was translated into Heaven. Enoch is a picture of the Raptured Church caught up into the Heavenly haven before the Tribulation disaster.

Genesis 5:22 introduces an event in the life of Enoch that revolutionized his relationship with God. God was prophetically revealing that an event of universally destructive proportions would occur at the time of Methuselah's decease.

The Biblical account reads in Genesis 5:22, "And Enoch walked with God after he begat Methuselah three hundred years.

Genesis 5:21 reveals that Enoch lived sixty-five years before Methuselah's birth, but obviously without achieving anything spiritually note-worthy. But with God's Revelation through Methuselah's birth came the transformation that shaped Enoch's life and led to his Divinely orchestrated exit. Genesis 5:24 records the translation of Enoch. "And Enoch walked with God:" and he was not; for God took him," or translated him before the Flood.

With Enoch's translation Methuselah "when gone so be it" continued his earthly sojourn. Yes, Methuselah's name meant, "when gone, so be it."

A mathematical Bible equation proves beyond a shadow of a doubt that the God-given fact of the coming Flood was revealed through Methuselah's name.

Genesis 5:25-32 reveals that Methuselah was 187 years old when Lamech was born and that Lamech was 182 when Noah was born. Adding the two numbers reveals that Methuselah was 369 years old when Noah was born. The Biblical passage of Genesis 7:6 reveals that Noah was 600 years old when the Flood came upon the earth. When adding 369 the age of Methuselah at Noah's birth, with 600 the age of Noah at the Flood, the conclusion is that Methuselah was 969 years old in the year of the Flood. Genesis 5:27 reveals that Methuselah, whose name meant "when gone: so be it," was 969 years old when he died. It, therefore, is concluded that Methuselah died in the year of the Flood, achieving the Revelation that God gave to Enoch.

Enoch's translation provides a vivid picture of the Church's Pre-Tribulation Rapture. Noah and his family's preservation through the Flood was a picture of a segment of Israel that God will supernaturally preserve through the Tribulation. Genesis 6:14 reveals the waterproof measures that God commanded Noah to "Seal" the ark. And thou shalt pitch (Seal) it within and without with pitch.

Revelation 7:2-4 reveals the ranks of the Divinely preserved through the Tribulation.

John's states, "and I saw another angel ascending from the east, having the seal of the living God: and he cried with a loud voice to the four angels, to whom it was given to hurt the earth and the sea, saying, Hurt not the earth neither the sea, nor the trees, till we have sealed the servants of our God in their foreheads. And I heard the number of them which were sealed: and there were sealed a hundred and forty and four thousand of all the tribes of the children of Israel."

So, Noah and his family's preservation through the Flood typically represents the 144,000 Jews preserved or sealed by God to pass through the Tribulation.

The segment of the ungodly destroyed in the Flood is illustrative of the ungodly who will die in the Tribulation period.

In analyzing the terms "Flood" as in Noah's day and "Tribulation" as in the Eschatological periods reveals the events' destructive correspondence.

The term "Flood" is the Greek word "KATAKLUSMOS," a deluge. It is the original term of the English word "cataclysm." A cataclysm is a violent change or upheaval, which certainly appropriately explicates the "Flood" destruction.

The term "Tribulation" as in the "Tribulation Period is the Greek word "THLIPSIS," which originates from the verb "THLIBO," which means "Press," a term used for pressing out grapes in a wine press. Thus, the term describes the activity of women and children as they trampled on grapes in a wine press, squeezing out the juice. The figures suggest the heavy pressures of life that sometimes become unbearable. Certainly, this correctly evaluates this period of unbearable-ness and the excruciating nature of that time.

But the saints need not be discombobulated because God promises a Rapture, a deliverance for His people. Revelation 3:10 voices the Church's Rapture message, "Because thou hast kept the word of my patience, I also will keep thee from the "hour of temptation," which shall come upon all the world, to try them that dwell upon the earth.

In I Thessalonians 1:9-10, Paul declares that Christ has delivered us from the "wrath to come."

The Book of Revelation chapter 4:1-2 presents the Church age's expiration and simultaneously the Tribulation period's inception, as signaled by the "Trumpet."

This trumpet blast has extensive signification in relation to comprehending God's Eschatological dealings.

1. It is a signal of regathering and deliverance to the Church. (I Thess. 4:16-17).
2. It is a dramatic signal to the Jews dispersed among the nations for their immediate mass return to Jerusalem. As expressed by the eagle-eyed prophet Isaiah in Isaiah 27:13, "And it shall come to pass in that day, that the great trumpet shall be blown, and they shall come which were ready to perish in the land of Assyria, and the outcasts in the land of Egypt, and shall worship the Lord in the holy mount at Jerusalem.
3. It signals a declaration of "war" during this post-Rapture period that will

culminate with a multitude of nations assembling in defeat in the battle of Armageddon. The prophet Joel expounds in Joel 2:1, "Blow ye the trumpet in Zion and sound an alarm in my holy mountain": let all the inhabitants of the land tremble: for the day of the Lord cometh, for it is nigh at hand. Joel continues with the same alarming theme in Joel 3:9-11 as he states, "Proclaim ye this among the Gentiles; Prepare war, wake up the mighty men, let all the men of war draw near; let them come up. Beat your plowshares into swords and your pruninghooks into spears: let the weak say, I am strong. Assemble yourselves, and come, all ye heathen, and gather yourselves together round about: thither cause thy mighty ones to come down, O Lord.

Simultaneously with the Heavenly "Judgment of the Believers Works," the horrendous 7-year Tribulation period begins on earth.

Revelation 5 records the Heavenly throne room scenario. Again, John was given a glimpse of God

Almighty, sitting on the Throne of Glory with a book in His right hand containing seven seals.

A strong angel proclaimed loudly, "Who is worthy to open the book, and to loose the seals thereof? No man in Heaven, on earth or under the earth was worthy."

The book held in the right hand of the Almighty was a "Biblion or a Scroll."

The seven seals reveal the secretive nature of God's culminative prophetical program.

A seal was a device often made with wax. An imprint pushed upon it forbade the unauthorized from opening. But once a seal was broken, it was impossible to repair without leaving unmistakable pieces of evidence of unauthorized tampering. Therefore, the suggestion of the intact seals is that man before this time has had no access or entrance into the concealed secrets of the seven seals.

In New Testament Times, Roman law required that a "will" be sealed seven times as a tampering preventative measure.

As the scroll was rolled up, it was sealed every turn or so seven times, and the seals were not to be broken until after the testator's death.

Truly providentially, Christ Jesus, "the heir of all things," comes forward, the Lion of the tribe of Judah as the only one worthy to open the seven seals. Therefore, Christ is revealed as the worthy Lamb because it is "He that hast redeemed us to God from every kindred and tongue and people and nation.

Daniel 9:27 describes the covenant of peace that the Antichrist will make with Israel and the nations prior to these seven years. A truce he will break at the three and one-half year segment.

Then in Revelation 6:19 is described in picturesque detail the successive features of the Tribulation period.

In chapter 6, Christ "the Lamb" opens the first six seals.

In each of the first four seals, a rider is presented on a horse of a different color.

The rider is presented as riding a white horse in the first seal. In Revelation chapter 19, Christ returns with His saints in victorious accomplishment riding a white horse. But in this instance, it is not a time of victory but judgment, doom, and disaster. The rider is obviously on impostor, the Antichrist attempting to duplicate the Messianic credentials. Jesus said in Matthew 24:5, "Many shall come in my name, saying I am Christ and shall deceive many."

The character of this horseman, when compared with Christ, is infinitely inferior. Christ, the triumphant rider of Revelation 19:12, wore "many crowns" (the diademata polla). In contrast, the Antichrist wore a single stephanos (wreath-crown) in the passage. Moreover, Christ possesses the "sharp sword" while the Antichrist has in his possession "a bow."

To view this horseman as Christ certainly reveals the delusive mission of the Antichrist who comes speaking of peace but brings" sudden destruction as travail upon a woman with child and they shall not escape."

In the second seal, John presents a rider on a red horse. This horseman was given "power to take peace from the earth."

That the inhabitants should kill one another, this Divine disclosure coincides with the visionary predictions of Jesus concerning "war and rumors of war" Matthew 24:6.

But the "red horse" reveals the unparalleled prevalency of war and bloodshed. It is not coincidental that the color of this horse is the color of blood. In the third seal, the prophet John reveals a rider on a "black horse," Revelation 6:5-6.

The rider on this black horse and a pair of balances in his hand. John heard a voice in the midst of the four beasts say, "A measure of wheat for a penny, and three measures of barley for a penny and see thou hurt not the oil and wine."

This rider on a "black horse" presents a time of unprecedented "famine" sweeping the nations with great acceleration.

The balance reveals the ancient method of selling food by weighing it on one side with a specific set of weights on the opposite side. Thus, the detrimental consequences of the universality of war (the red horse) result in the universality of famine (the black horse).

The "penny" in this passage is the word "DENARIUS," which was a silver coin worth about $3.62. A denarius represented a day's wages for a soldier in Caesar Augustus' army. The passage declares that the inflationary economy of the Tribulation period will be so outlandish that a man will spend an entire day's pay for a loaf or measure of bread.

In this period, the oil and wine of the wealthy are not hurt, but in Revelation 6:15, the prohibition is removed.

The opening of the fourth seal reveals a rider on a pale horse.

The term "pale" means "pale green or yellow-green."

The rider on this "pale green or yellow-green" horse is identified as "Death," and "Hell" follows with him. And power was given to this rider over the fourth part of the earth, (Revelation 6:8) to kill with the sword, and with hunger, and with death, and with the beasts of the earth.

The term the fourth part of the "earth" may signify death's vast effect over an area equal to one-quarter of the earth's landmass. The term "earth" is the Greek word "GE" associated with our English word "GEOLOGY," which deals with "earth" science.

The term "the fourth part of the earth" signifies the judgmental annihilation of one-fourth of the earth's population, based upon the current population of some 7.7 billion people. In that case, approximately 1.925 billion will die.

Revelation 6:9-11 is revealed the opening of the fifth seal, a time of great "Martyrdom" during the last three and one half year segment of the Tribulation period. In this fifth seal, John saw the souls under the altar of those who will be killed during the Tribulation period for the "Word of their Testimony and who loved not their lives unto the death (Revelation 12:11). The unison plea of this Tribulation group of martyrs before God is "How long, O Lord, holy and true, dost thou not judge and avenge our Blood on them that dwell on the earth? The Divine answer to this group of Godly martyrs is " that they should rest yet for a little season, until their fellowservants also, and their brethren, that should be killed as they were, should be fulfilled."

As the sixth seal opens in Revelation 6:12-17, it is characterized by catastrophic physical and visible changes on earth and in heavenly bodies. In a great earthquake, the sun becomes as a black sackcloth of hair, and the moon becomes like blood. Also, the stars of Heaven fell upon the earth, and every mountain and island were moved out of their places.

To corroborate this futuristic happening of the earth, every mountain, and island moving out of its place, scientists are already acknowledging the fact that the earth's crust moves.

An encyclopedia report on "The Drifting Continent" reports that the earth consists of a liquid core with a radius of about 2,170 miles, a mantle about 1800 miles thick, and a crust. Their theory is that movements in the Earth's mantle are causing continental drifts. For example, scientists have found that Asia and Africa are splitting apart along a large fault in the center of the Red Sea.

As a result of the catastrophic changes, the kings, the great men, the rich, the chief captains, the mighty men, and every bondman and freeman hid themselves in the dens and the rocks of the mountains.

This detrimentally affected group cried out to the mountains and rocks, "Fall on us and hides us from the face of Him that sitteth on the throne and from the wrath of the Lamb. For the great day of His wrath is come, and who shall be able to stand.

Between the sixth and seventh seals in Revelation 7 is revealed a group of 144,000 Jews-12,000 from each tribe who are supernaturally "SEALED" to preserve them through the Tribulation tragedies.

Revelation chapter 14:1 reveals the nature of the "SEAL," as being that of having the Father's name "SEALED" in their foreheads.

The first four seals presented the judgment of the four horsemen. The opening of the seventh seal reveals the judgment of the seven trumpets.

The utilization of the seven trumpets as judgmental annunciators or indicators causes us Biblically to recapitulate the children of Israel's possessive acquisition of the city of Jericho in Joshua chapter 6. For it was on the seventh day that Israel compassed the walls of Jericho 7 times, blew the trumpet, the walls fell, and Israel took the city.

Similarly, the seven trumpets of the 7th seal declare judgment. In Revelation 8:1, as this 7th seal is initially opened, silence occurs in Heaven for 30 minutes. However, this silence doesn't last as judgment occurs in universally catastrophic proportions. Seven angelic beings successively sound the seven trumpets.

As the first angel sounds the trumpet in Revelation 8:7, the resultant consequence is hail and fire mingled with blood cast upon the earth. One-third of the trees and all the green grass are burnt up.

But in this passage, one-third of the entire earth is on fire, causing destruction through burning, oxygen deprivation, and lack of vegetation for sustaining life.

The second trumpet sounds and its destructive results are recorded with great details (Revelation 8:8-9).

In this judgment, John sees a great mountain of fire cast into the sea resulting in one-third of the sea becoming blood, one-third of the sea creatures dying, and one-third of the ships being destroyed. Certainly, a judgment of this nature and magnitude will be great, devastating to the world water transportation system since the world's merchant fleet totals almost 54,000 ships. Moreover, if the nearly 4,000 navy ships of the world are added, the sum total is 58,000 vessels. Therefore, one-third of the destruction of vessels, based upon the present figures, would destroy over 17,000 ships.

In addition to this, the 4,000 navy ships are crewed by approximately 1,527,000 personnel. Therefore, based upon this present figure, over 500,000 personnel will die.

The third angel (trumpet sounds) in Revelation 8:10-11, and the result is that a great star called "Wormwood" fell from Heaven, falling upon one-third of the earth's water. The result is that the affected waters became "Wormwood." The term "Wormwood" refers to a bitter and intoxicating plant and symbolized hardships and the evils of life in the old Testament.

This judgment against the earth's sanitation results in the death of many as the waters are polluted with bitterness and harmful effects.

The fourth trumpet judgment sounds in Revelation 8:12-13, causing one-third of the sun, the moon, and the stars to be darkened. How devastating to those dependent on solar energy.

John is also warned in verse 13 that three woes or trumpet judgments are to come. The fifth trumpet judgment (Revelation 9:1-12) opens in verse 1, with a "star" falling from Heaven upon the earth. The fact that a key is given to "him" (the star) reveals that the star is not a planetary body but an angel.

This angel (star) opens the bottomless pit in verse 2, and there arose a smoke out of the pit, comparative to the smoke of a great furnace. The smoke was so all-encompassing that the sun and the air were darkened.

The term "bottomless pit" is an abyss or a great shaft. Luke 8:31 reveals the dreadful nature of this place as the demons expressed fear that Jesus might send them there.

In this passage, out of the abyss of smoke emerges locusts (verse 3-9) upon the earth, which have the power of the scorpions of the earth.

The locusts are anomalous monstrosities deviating from the regular locust dietary consumption, which feed on vegetation. For these locusts are forbidden to hurt the grass or any green thing but are commanded to hurt only those men who have not the protective seal of God in their foreheads.

The locusts have the power to torment, as the torment of a scorpion when he striketh a man. During these five months of locust torment, men will seek and desire to die and shall not be able to.

In this passage, the term for locust is "AKRIS," meaning locust or grasshoppers. The terrible power given to these creatures is revealed by the reference to them having the power of scorpions.

The scorpion is a member of the arachnids of hot or tropical regions - creature 4 to 7 inches in diameter including the leg spread, with large pincers at the front of the body and also a curving, fierce sting laden tail.

Imagine the terrorism, the emotional and physical pain of this creature with the mobility of a grasshopper, and the harmful sting of a scorpion inflicting the ungodly for five long, unrelenting months.

Revelation 9:11 reveals that these torment equipped locust-scorpions, who have the shape of horses, on their heads are crowns like gold, who have the faces of men, hair like women's, teeth like a lion, breastplates like iron, and tails like a scorpion, that the name of their king is Abaddon or Apollyon" which means destroyer. It is this destroyer that sends his emissaries with deleterious intentions.

The sixth angel (trumpet) sounds (Revelation 9:13-21), and John hears a voice commanding four angels to be released, which are bound in the River Euphrates.

This command is mysteriously connected with the appearance of an army of 200 million horsemen who destroy one-third of the earth's population. Note that the world's population has exploded to approximately 7.7 billion souls. So predicated on this figure, 2.6 billion people will die. And according to the 2020 figure, the current population of China is over 1.4 billion.

Combining this mass annihilation with that of the fourth seal, over half of the world's population will die when one-fourth of humanity dies. Thus, an army of 200 million soldiers seems highly preposterous or largely ludicrous until it is realized that the Chinese, in a television documentary, have been reported to have boasted of a people's army of 200 million militiamen as far back as 1972.

The mass killings of this age are instigated by demonic fluence. The riders (Revelation 9:17-19) in this 200 million-member army have breastplates of fire, Jacinth, and brimstone. So also, the heads of the horses were as the heads of lions and out of their mouths issued fire and smoke and brimstone.

Sadly, it is characteristic of the survivors of this tragedy that repentance is absent. As Revelation 9:21 reports, "Neither repented they of their murders, nor of their sorceries, nor of their fornication, nor of their thefts."

Revelation 11:3-14 introduces two witnesses thrust into the limelight of worldwide dynamic visibility for 1260 days or three and one-half years of the Tribulation Period.

The witnesses are Divinely equipped with power for doing. The witnesses are compared to two olive trees that produce oil, a symbol of the Holy Ghost, and two lampstands or candlesticks giving light to a sin-darkened world.

Revelation 11:5 reveals the indestructible preservation of the two witnesses during this period, for if any will hurt them, fire proceedeth out of their mouth and devoureth their enemies (Revelation 11:3-5).

Students of Biblical investigation have speculated for decades concerning the identity of the two witnesses.

The Bible states in Revelation 11:6 that the two witnesses during this 3 1/2 period of their ministry "have power to shut Heaven, that it rain not in the days of their prophecy." This ability bears an unmistakable resemblance to the ministry of Elijah. Through God's supernatural power, he shut up Heaven eliminating rain for the same period, 3 1/2 years or 42 months.

The witnesses (Revelation 11:6) also possess "power over waters to turn them to blood, and to smite the earth with all plagues, as often as they will." This miraculous demonstration duplicates the ministry of Moses in the Egyptian plagues, the waters were turned to blood, and other plagues against the Egyptians occurred.

Therefore, it is the general consensus of Biblical scholars that Moses and Elijah are the two witnesses prophesied.

Revelation 11:7 reveals the fact that when the witnesses reach the end of their period of ministry. "that the beast that ascendeth out of the bottomless pit shall make war against them, and shall overcome them, and kill them."

Revelation 11:8-10 records that the two witnesses shall be slain in the city which spiritually is called Sodom and Egypt. This city is obviously Jerusalem because, in verse 8, it is identified as the city "where also our Lord was crucified."

The demoralized people of the world, obviously through television, will view the godless execution of the witnesses with no trace of sorrow or grief.

Still, they "shall rejoice over them, and make merry, and shall send gifts one to another," This is the only time that rejoicing is mentioned in the Tribulation period and tragically here in connection with persecution and: martyrdom.

But after 3 1/2 days, the two witnesses who are on display as trophies of the Antichrist's supposed superiority are resurrected into Heaven, causing fear to fall on the astounded viewing audience.

Then God displays His genuine superior power (verses 11-12) as a great earthquake devastatingly erupts in Jerusalem, killing one-tenth of the city.

The remnant, therefore, "were affrighted and gave glory to the God of heaven."

The second woe is past, and behold, the third woe cometh quickly (Revelation 11:14). In Revelation 11:15, the seventh angel (trumpet): sounds resulting in great voices in Heaven saying, "The kingdoms of this world are become the kingdoms of our Lord and of His Christ; and He shall reign forever and ever." Though not immediately established, the expected kingdom is forecasted with great anticipatory jubilation.

The vision of the 24 elders in verses 15-16 demonstrates their humbled reaction as they fell upon their faces and worshipped God.

In verses 15-19, God provides a panorama of His future events as though they were already present. Then, in verses 15-17, the establishment of Christ's worldwide reign, the judgment of the raging nations at Armageddon, the judgment of the dead (20:11-15) when the destroyers of the earth will be destroyed and the rewarding of the prophets and saints in millennial positions of rule and dominion, (20:4-6).

Revelation chapters 12–13 vividly portrays the seven personages who play key roles in this latter Tribulation era.

In this middle portion of the Tribulation period recorded in Revelation 12:1-2, a great wonder appears in Heaven, a woman clothed with the sun and the moon under her feet and a crown of twelve stars upon her head.

The woman was pregnant with a child, travailing in birth to be delivered. The woman portrayed very obviously represents Israel. For Joseph in Genesis 37:9 received a dream from God concerning the sun, the moon, and the 11 stars making obeisance to him. When Joseph is added to his brethren depicted through the celestial bodies, the 12 tribes were prophetically portrayed.

The travail that victimized the woman is the Great Tribulation, which is excruciatingly presented through the Biblical symbol of birth. The birth process was graphically used with commonality in the old Testament to depict acute suffering, especially the time of Jacob's trouble (Jeremiah 30:5-7).

In Revelation 12:3-4, the second personage is presented, which is a great red dragon. The dragon in this passage is revealed in verse 9, as the old serpent: (Genesis 3:1-10) also called the Devil or Satan which deceiveth the whole world.

In verse 3 reveals this dragon as possessing seven heads, ten horns, and seven crowns upon his head.

The ten horns corroborate the prophecies of Daniel 7:7,20, 24 and Revelation 17:12 concerning the ten leader confederation that operates in satanic coalescence with the Antichrist, in the end-time against Israel.

The destructive designs of the dragon are revealed in Revelation 12:4. For it was the Devil who agitated Herod to attempt to kill the Christ child as reported in Matthew chapter 2.

Revelation 12:5 gives a synoptic view of the third personage (Christ), who is depicted through the illustration of a child.

God's Divine intentions concerning Christ are revealed through four Christological realities. (1) Christ's birth, (2) Christ's destiny of reducing to futility all His foes, (3) His ascension, and (4) His destiny of enthronement. Finally, Revelation 12:6 reveals the woman's (Israel's) flight into the wilderness to a place Divinely prepared by God.

The passage reveals that Israel is sustained in this locality of safety for the latter 3 ½ years of the Tribulation period.

Many believe that the place of safety will be located at "Petra." Petra is the natural rock fortification south of Israel that, in antiquities, was the capital of Edom.

The city Petra is one of the most inaccessible places on the face of the earth, primarily because it is built in a deep basin or plain High in the mountains and is surrounded by granite and sandstone cliffs.

The only entrance to the city is by "the Sik," a narrow, six-tenths of a mile-long gorge between towering red granite cliffs. It, therefore, provides an impregnable asylum.

In Revelation 12:7-12, the fourth personage, Michael the archangel, is courageously portrayed. Michael the archangel is consistently employed by God as the angelic protectorate of the Jewish people (Daniel 12:1). This passage provides the post-fight analysis of the war in the heavenlies between Michael and his angels and the Devil and his angels. Michael, empowered by God, is the unquestioned winner.

As a result, the Devil who previously had access to Heaven for accountability purposes was expulsed to the earth during this mid-point of the Tribulation.

Revelation 12:11-13 reveals the Devil's destructive purposes, but also God's people's preservation, "For they overcame him (the Devil) by the blood of the Lamb, and by the Word of their testimony.".. Revelation 12:17 presents the Devil's anger because of the escape of the woman (Israel) to the place of safety (Petra).

The evil one's anger is then outrageously expressed against the fifth personage," the remnant of Israel."

Revelation 13:1-10 describes the sixth personage of this latter Tribulation Period. The personage is called "the beast."

John, in verse 1, describes the emergence of "the beast" as coming out of "the sea." The Terminology sea is used elsewhere to indicate the nations of the earth. As Revelation 17:15 explains, "The waters which thou sawest, where the whore sitteth, are people, and multitudes, and nations, and tongues. Therefore, a strong possibility exists that this leader of universal prominence will be a gentile.

Verse 2 describes the beast (Antichrist) as having seven heads and ten horns and upon the horns ten crowns.

The Biblical significance of the number seven is perfection or completeness.

But the Antichrist who epitomizes imperfection demonstrates a deviation from the number seven's prophetic symbolism.

The seven heads may indicate in this passage the beast's worldwide dominion over the seven continental landmasses of our globe: North America, South America, Europe, Asia, Africa, Australia, and Antarctica.

The ten horns are described in Revelation 17:12 as "... ten kings, which have received no kingdom as yet; but receive power as kings one hour with the beast."

When this passage is viewed jointly with Daniel's worldwide kingdom prophetical vision, in Daniel chapter 2, it is evident that the ten toes of Daniel's image correspond with the ten horns of this passage. In each, the indication is of a ten-nation confederation which many believe is some European last days peaceful nations resurgence group.

Revelation 13:2 also describes "the beast as possessing the collective attributes in his personage of the great worldwide kingdom described in Daniel chapter 7 – the characteristics of the lion (Babylon), the bear (Medo-Persians) and the leopard (Grecians).

Verse 2 also describes the Antichrist as being energized by the dragon (the Devil). Finally, in verse 3, the Antichrist employs his satanic lying wonders by amazingly being healed from a deadly wound. The result is the hypnotic captivation of the masses.

Verse 4 reveals the mass worship of the dragon and the beast. As corroborated by II Thessalonians 2:4, which states that he opposeth and exalteth himself above all that is called God, or that is worshipped: so that he as God sitteth in the temple of God, shewing himself that he is God.

Verse 5-6 reveals that the Antichrist speaketh great things and blasphemes against God, against God's tabernacle and the heavenly residents. Like other leaders such as Hitler, the Antichrist will be a gifted, captivating orator.

In Daniel 9:27, the Antichrist era of dominion is revealed to be seven years. But in the middle of his peace treaty, he breaks the agreement, as confirmed by Revelation 13:5.

In Revelation 13:7, the Antichrist makes war with the saints and gains power over the kindred, tongues, and nations.

In Revelation 13:10, he leadeth them into captivity and killeth with the sword.

Revelation 13:11-18 presents the seventh personage of the latter Tribulation era.

He is the Antichrist's chief accomplice in the Devil's destructive and seductive scheme to destroy mankind.

He is called "another beast" in Revelation 13:11. He is described as "coming up out of the earth," referring to this beast's Jewish descent.

The deceptive nature of this beast is revealed in verse 11, as "he had two horns like a lamb." In verse 8, Christ is alluded to as "the Lamb," so the apparent intent is to falsely duplicate Christ's personage.

But verse 11 also states this beast speaks "like a dragon," the Devil. Verse 12-18 reveals that this beast causeth or persuadeth mankind to worship the first beast who was healed of the deadly wound.

This second beast miraculously, "maketh fire come down from Heaven.

He utilizes his deceptive miracles to influence the people to make an image of the beast. He possesses the power to give life or animation to the first beast's image, causing the image to speak, and he kills all who will not worship the Antichrist.

"He causeth all," regardless of the economic category or social position, both small and great, rich and poor, free and bond to receive a mark in their right hand or their foreheads.

And that no man might buy or sell, save he that had the mark, the name of the beast, or the number of his name.

Revelation 13:18 states the number of the beast: for it is the number of a man: and his number is six hundred threescore and six (666).

Truly, we live in a significantly numerically orientated society with social security numbers, zip codes, electronic banking, and electronic price takeover codes. A system ready for the Antichrist's exploitation.

The number 666 causes Biblical scholars to recollect the statue of King Nebuchadnezzar's manufacture and worship in Daniel 3:1, which was 60 by 6 cubits. If it were an obelisk of the usual type, it would have had a square base, and hence it would be 60 X 6 X 6 cubits.

The number 666 of Revelation 13:18 may convey man's imperfection, which falls short of God's perfection, as illustrated by the number 7.

Revelation 14:9-13 reveals God as a Divine retributive reactionary against the Antichrist worshippers.

Verse 10 pronounces the doom on the Antichrist's worshippers and those who worship his image and receive the mark (666).

Firstly, they shall drink of the wine of the wrath of God, which is poured out without mixture into the cup of His indignation.

The signification of "poured out without mixture" literally conveys a mixture unmixed, no dilution, or God's wrath in full strength.

Secondly, they "shall be tormented with fire and brimstone in the presence of holy angels and the presence of the Lamb.

To be tormented with fire and brimstone reveals the undefinable suffering of these children of perdition. For brimstone is burning sulfur, a chemical that causes continual pain.

In Revelation chapter 16:1-12, six of the seven vial judgments occur.

The first vial judgment consists of a plague reminiscent of Egypt's sixth plague, in Exodus 9:8-12.

The plague (16:1-2) is exclusively poured out on the Antichrist's followers, who take the mark of the beast and worship his image.

This judgment involves the judgment of "noisome and grievous sores" on this satanic coalition.

Edgar C. James, in his book, "Day of the Lamb," describes the sores as loathsome and malignant.

The second vial involves causing the sea to become like a dead man's blood, resulting in the death of every living soul in the sea.

The third vial judgment results in the rivers and the fountain of waters being turned into blood.

The second trumpet judgment will result in the third part of the sea becoming blood. The third trumpet results in the third part of the inland waters becoming bitter as wormwood. But in the second and third vials, the earth's entire water supply becomes blood.

The fourth vial (16:8-9) occurs as the fourth angel pours out his bowl of judgment upon the sun resulting in man being "scorched with fire."

Imagine the unrelenting burning sensations in the absence of pure water to soothe the victims.

The evil nature of the victims is evidentially apparent as they blaspheme God's name.

The fifth vial (16:10-11) brings the judgment directly upon the throne of the Antichrist, causing darkness throughout his entire kingdom, possibly centralized in Jerusalem.

The people gnaw their tongues in pain but cease not to blaspheme God's wonderful name.

The sixth vial (16:12) involves the drying up of the River Euphrates to prepare a means of suitable travel for the kings of the east.

The Euphrates River has global strategic importance. Africa, Palestine, and Arabia are to the southwest of this river, and Russia, China, access India, and Iran are to its northeast.

Therefore, the drying up of this body of water extends some; 1700 miles flowing southeast into the Persian Gulf, providing easy access for the armies coming into Israel for Armageddon.

In ancient times the Euphrates was a natural barrier to invading armies of the east. But with this catastrophe, the barrier is removed, and the eastern armies will invade like a flood.

The seventh vial of this climactic phase of the Tribulation (16:17 21) involves a Heavenly announcement from the throne that, "It is done." The result is voices, thunders, lightning, and an earthquake of such proportions, not seen in the history of mankind.

The great city, presumably Jerusalem, is divided into three parts (11:18).

A judgment of hailstones weighing 100 pounds falls from Heaven, but the ungodly persist in blaspheming God.

Chapters 17-18 provide a glimpse into the fall of ecclesiastical Babylon. Chapter 17:5 describes this Babylon as "The Great, The Mother of Harlots and Abominations of the Earth."

This religious, social, economic, anti-God, anti-Christ system derives its name from the consolidated group's defiance against God in Genesis 11:1-9.

It is the Babylon of antiquities that has given birth to all false religions. Therefore, it is a system of spiritual and moral obstinacy that God is bound to break.

5

THE BATTLE OF ARMAGEDDON AND CHRIST'S SECOND COMING

At the climax of the Great Tribulation period, the earth is in total disarray because of the satanic tripartite's vicious afflictions.

Though the earthly situation will be chaotic, the heavenly realm will be filled with incomparable ecstasy.

In a secure and inviolable relationship, the Church is presently engaged to Christ.

In ancient times after the engagement period when the marriage was to be finalized, the Bridegroom would go to the bride's house and claim her for his wife.

Then after the wedding, the Bridegroom would take her to his house for a wedding supper, lasting as long as one week. Chapter 19:5-10 records this event. Finally, chapter 19:11-16 at the time of the Tribulation closing presents what is commonly called Christ's Second Advent.

In discussing the Coming of the Lord, it must be understood that it is a subject of two phases. (1) The Coming of the Lord for His saints prior to the Tribulation and (2) the Coming of the Lord with His saints to establish His kingdom upon earth.

The first phase of the Lord's coming is called the "Rapture," an event happening with such secrecy that it occurs as a "thief in the night" (I Thessalonians 5:2). This second phase of the Second Coming will be an event of public visibility. As Revelation 1:7 describes, "Behold He cometh with clouds and every eye shall see Him, and they also which pierced Him: and all kindreds of the earth shall wail because of Him. The prophet Zechariah in Zechariah 14:1-3 describes this time when the nations will encompass Israel with destructive intentions. He states with prophetic accuracy God's Revelation, "For I will gather all nations against Jerusalem to battle; and the city shall be taken and the house rifled, and the women ravished.... Zechariah states that the end-time events of world history are inextricably connected with Jerusalem.

The importance of Israel and Jerusalem may be obscured to the spiritually blind and desensitized. But the Devil recognizes their importance in God's culminative world program.

The song of Moses (Deut. 32:8) explains how God mysteriously, spiritually, and geographically revolved His Divine program around Israel. The passage states, "When the Most High divided to the nations their inheritance, when He separated the sons of Adam, He set the bounds of the people according to the number of the children of Israel." Thus, the Bible declares that the size of the nations of the world and their growth through acquisitive conquests is all based upon the Jewish world population. Therefore, God providentially has placed Israel in a strategically locational position. Ezekiel 38:12 (ASV marg. note) and He calls it "the navel or center of the earth."

"As the navel is set in the center of the human body so is the land of Israel the center of the world and Jerusalem is the center of Israel, and the sanctuary in the center of Jerusalem, and the holy place in the center of the sanctuary; and the ark is in the center of the Holy Place, and the foundation stone before the holy place because from it the world was founded. (This exposed rock over which the Dome of the Rock is built is called "the foundation stone)." In addition to the Devil's hatred of Israel because of God's usage of her in His Divine program. The nations covet Israel because of the economic treasures in the Dead Sea.

The Dead Sea (Salt Sea), which is 1286 feet below sea level, the lowest spot on the face of the earth, contains an ever-growing residue of salt and other precious minerals.

It has been estimated that the "potash," a valuable fertilizer needed for vegetation and animal life, is so richly resident that there is enough "potash" to supply the entire world's needs for 2,000 years.

The value of the mineral deposits in the Dead Sea has been estimated at more than the combined wealth of some countries while being estimated at one trillion dollars at one time by evaluators. Revelation 19:11 reveals the descension of Christ from Heaven for this visible, public arrival.

Christ arrives on a "white horse," "a symbol of purity and victory. Verse 11 reveals His unfailing character - "Faithful and true." Verse 12 reveals His eyes as a flame of fire, the many crowns on His head, and His new name, which is undisclosed.

Verse 13 reveals Christ adorned in His redemptive garments, "and He was clothed with a vesture dipped in blood, and His name is called The Word of God."

Acts 1:9-12 records the miraculous event of Jesus' departure from the earth after His redemptive resurrection accomplishment.

As Christ departed, two men (angels) stood by in white apparel and proclaimed this same Jesus, which is taken up from you into Heaven, so come in like manner as ye have seen Him go into Heaven. The place of Jesus' exit was the mount called "Olivet," also called "Olives."

The Biblical account states that the same place where Jesus' feet left the earth will also touch the earth (Mount of Olives) at His Revelation. As substantiated by Zechariah 14:3-4, "Then shall the Lord go forth, and fight against those nations, as when he fought in the day of battle. And his feet shall stand in that day upon the mount of Olives, which is before Jerusalem on the east, and the mount of Olives shall cleave in the midst thereof toward the east and toward the west, and there shall be a very great valley; and half of the mountain shall remove toward the north, and half of it toward the south."

Imagine this mountain that is a flattened, rounded ridge, compositionally is of cretaceous limestone formation, that in length is over a mile forming the highest level of the range of hills to the east of Jerusalem, that rises 250 feet higher than the Temple mount, will be split in two when Jesus steps down on it.

It is interesting to note that an oil company doing seismic studies has discovered a gigantic fault running east and west precisely through the center of Mount Olives, so severe it could split at any time. But the mountain cannot split yet, for it is waiting for the touchdown of Jesus' feet.

Jesus' arrival with His saints in the Second Coming is necessitated by the convergence of the beast (19:19) and the kings of the earth. They consolidated to fight Israel in the battle of Armageddon.

Revelation 16:12 provides a forecast or preview of that battle as being made possible by the drying up of the Euphrates, allowing the kings of the east access into Palestine. But this passage in Revelation chapter 19 provides the chronology of Armageddon concerning the succession of end-time events.

Armageddon comes from two Hebrew words, "Har Megiddo," meaning "the hill of Megiddo" - a term extraordinarily appropriate for geography with such militaristic historicity and ultimate destiny. "Megiddo" means "place of troops" or "place of slaughter."

It is at the foot of this Mount Megiddo, also called the Plain of Esdraelon or the Valley of Jezreel, that decisive incidents such as the victory of Deborah and Barak over Sisera (Judges 5:19-20), Gideon's defeat of Midian (Judges 6:33), Saul's death at the hands of the Philistines (I Sam. 31, II Sam.4:4) and Josiah's death in battle with Pharoh Neco (II Kings 23:29-30) all took place.

Revelation 19:14 describes Christ and the armies of Heaven upon white horses, clothed in fine linen, white and clean (righteous).

Revelation 19:15 reveals that "out of His mouth goeth a sharp sword, that with it He should smite the nations. Paul in II Thessalonians 2:8 describes the same event, "And then shall the Wicked be revealed, whom the Lord shall consume with the spirit of His mouth and shall destroy with the brightness of His coming.

Revelation 19:15 describes Christ's retribution upon the ungodly and ..."He treadeth the winepress of the fierceness and wrath of Almighty God."

Revelation 19:16 reveals that Christ hath a name written on His vesture and His thigh, "King of Kings and Lord of Lords."

Revelation 19:17 describes the angelic invitation to the fowls of the air, the scavenger birds to feast at this massacre of the ungodly resistant troops. The invitation states expressly, "Come and gather your self together unto the supper of the great God. The book of Matthew 24

corroborates, "For wheresoever the carcass is there will the eagles be gathered together." Some believe that the eagles may refer to carnivorous vultures that voraciously eat dead carcasses.

During this battle, the scavengers will have more than enough to eat for according to Revelation 14:20, the "blood came out of the winepress, even unto the horse's bridle (four and one-half feet deep) for the space of 200 miles. Ezekiel 39:12

reveals that the death of the Antichrist's nations of confederation will be so enormous that it will require seven months to bury their dead.

Ezekiel 39:9 reveals that the weaponry, the shields, bucklers, the bows and arrows, the hand staves, and the spears shall be leftover in such an enormous supply that it will take seven years to burn them up.

Revelation 19:20 reveals the fate of the beast and his false prophet defeated by Christ's prolific return.

Both the beast and his false prophet, both of them, will be "cast alive into the lake of fire burning with brimstone.

6

THE MILLENNIUM

The Lord's coming with His saints effectively defeats the Antichrist, the false prophet, and the Devil.

In Revelation 19:20, the beast and the false prophet are cast into "the lake of fire," as its first inhabitants.

Then in Revelation 20:1-3, the Devil, already defeated by Christ Jesus, is cast into the bottomless pit, shut up with a seal, to deceive the nations no more till the thousand years should be fulfilled.

At this time, the martyrs of the Tribulation Period are resurrected as Revelation 20:4 states, "and they lived and reigned with Christ a thousand years."

It is important to understand that Christ's Second Coming was not just to fight the ungodly but also to establish His Millennium Kingdom or reign (Revelation 20:4).

The term "Millennium" originates from two Latin words, "MILLE" (thousand) and "ANNUM" (year), and is used to describe the Biblical golden age of Christ's 1,000-year reign on earth with His redeemed of the ages.

Mankind has fantasized and dreamed of a golden age, a time of utopian, idealistic realizations, to cause a cessation: of man's insurmountable difficulties, caused by the reverberating or the ever echoing effects of sin.

Romans 8:19-23 reveals that such a mental excursion of fantasy does not constitute candidacy for admission to an insane asylum but is a realistic ultimate provision for every child of God.

In Romans 8:19, the Apostle Paul expounds on the desire of all of creation to be delivered from sins disabling effects. He states, "the earnest expectation of the creature waiteth for the manifestation of the sons of God.

Then in Romans 8:21, he promises that all of creation shall be liberated from sin's enslavement." Because the creature (creation) itself shall be delivered from the bondage of corruption into the glorious liberty of the children of God."

This era of the Millennium will be an age of "Theocratic" or "Theocracy" government through Christ Jesus' personal governing. As Luke 1:30-33 elaborates concerning Christ's dominion that, "He shall be great and shall be called the Son of the Highest, and the Lord God shall give unto Him the Throne of His Father David. It is a time in which Jerusalem will be the central seat of the government as, Isaiah 24:23 reveals, the Lord of host shall reign in mount Zion and Jerusalem.

The Millennium will be a time of universal peace as the instruments of war are modified into instruments of agriculture as corroborated in Isaiah 2:4, "and they shall beat their swords into plowshares, and their spears into pruninghooks: nation shall not lift up sword against nation, neither shall they learn war anymore."

A time when the animal kingdom will be sensibly restored from their nature of ferocity produced by the fall of man.

As Isaiah 11:6-9 explains, "The wolf also shall dwell with the lamb, and the leopard shall lie down with the kid; and the calf and the young lion and the fatling together; and a little child shall lead them. And the cow and the bear shall feed; their young ones shall lie down together: and the lion shall eat straw like the ox. And the sucking child shall play on the hole of the asp, and the weaned child shall put his hand on the cockatrice' den. They shall not hurt nor destroy in all my holy mountain: for the earth shall be full of the knowledge of the Lord, as the waters cover the sea."

A time of prolongation of human life tantamount to the antediluvian period.

As Isaiah 65:20 states, "There shall be no more thence an infant of days, nor an old man that hath not filled his days: for the child shall die a hundred years old; but the sinner being an hundred years old shall be accursed."

Isaiah 65:22 further expounds that "for as the days of a tree are the days of my people, and (God says) mine elect shall long enjoy the work of their hands.

It is time in which the Dead Sea, which presently is 31 miles long, 9 to 10 miles wide, and its surface is approximately 1385 feet below sea level, will go through a dramatic transformation.

Presently, the Dead Sea has no exit for its waters except through evaporation. Also, its elemental composition makes it impossible for living things to dwell in it.

At this time, its "waters shall be healed" (Ezekiel 47:8). Its waters shall come alive as Ezekiel 47:9 states, "that everything that liveth, which moveth, whithers soever the rivers shall come, shall live: and there shall be a very great multitude of fish, because these waters shall come thither: for they shall be healed: and everything shall live whither the river cometh."

Ezekiel 47:12 also records the miraculous productivity of fruit during this time, for "by the river upon the bank thereof on this side and on that side, shall grow all trees for meat, whose leaf shall not fade, neither shall the fruit thereof be consumed: it shall bring forth new fruit according to his months because their waters they issued out of the sanctuary, and the fruit thereof shall be for meat, and the leaf thereof for medicine."

A time in which the desert will be effectively transformed, as Isaiah 35:1 reveals, "and the desert shall rejoice, and blossom as a rose."

A time in which sickness will be virtually eradicated for Isaiah 33:24 states, "and the inhabitants shall not say, I am sick.

It will be a time in which the land of Palestine will return to its former status of being "a land that flows with milk and honey." As the prophet Joel, in Joel 3:18, inspirationally predicts that "in that day, that the mountains shall drop down new wine, and the hills shall flow with milk." The terms "new wine" and "flow with milk" obviously refer to the abundance of viticulture (grapes) and productive pastures for sustaining vast cattle herds of milk cows.

It will be a time of the sevenfold increase of light (Isaiah 30:26).

An age in which farming will be pleasurable, because of the removal of the curse as Isaiah 55:13 reports, "Instead of the briar shall come up the myrtle tree. It is an age in which the Gentile nations of the world will be granted admission into the Kingdom according to their treatment of the Jewish nation (Matthew 25:31-46, Joel 3:1,2).

With such an age of peace, prosperity, restoration, and a God-controlled "Theocracy," ultimately to be established, the prayers of every child of God should be, "Lord thy kingdom come, Thy will be done."

THE NEW HEAVEN AND THE NEW EARTH

The Biblical passage reveals that at the expiration of the Millennium, the era of Christ's reign (1,000 years) upon the earth, the Devil bound in the bottomless pit for 1,000 years will revolt one last time.

As Revelation 20:7 prophecies, "and when the thousand years are expired, Satan shall be loosed out of his prison.

This deceiver incites an insurrection employing multitudes from "the four corners of the earth." . . together to battle: the number of whom is as the sand of the sea (Revelation 20:8).

Then with this group compassing Jerusalem, God delivers His peoples and "the beloved city" by sending "fire down from God out of heaven and devoured them" (Revelation 20:9).

With this rebellion overthrown, the Devil, who is defeated again by God, is cast into the lake of fire and brimstone; where the beast and the false prophet are and shall be tormented day and night forever and ever.

Then Revelation 20:11-15 presents an occasion called the White Throne of Judgment.

It is a time of reckoning and accountability in which the ungodly of the ages must come before the throne of God.

Revelation 20:5 reveals that this judgment occurs at the expiration of Christ's 1,000, year reign and after Satan's final rebellion. AS the passage states, "But the rest of the dead lived not again until the thousand years were finished."

It is a time when "the small and the great stand before God," as the ungodly are judged of those things written in the books, according to their works (Revelation 20:12).

And the sea gave up the dead which were in it; and death and hell delivered up the dead which were in them: and they were judged every man according to their works. (Revelation 20:13).

Then, "death and hell were cast into the lake of fire. This is the second death. And whosoever was not found written in the book of life was cast into the lake of fire.

Then Revelation 21:1 foretells the appearance of the new Heaven and the new earth. He states, "and I saw a new heaven and a new earth: for the first Heaven and the first earth were passed away, and there was no more sea.

The epistle of II Peter 3:10-13 describes how the transition will take place to effectuate the transformation of a new heaven and a new earth.

In II Peter 3:10, Peter states, that "the heavens shall pass away with a great noise, and the elements shall melt with fervent heat, the earth also and the works that are therein shall be burned up.

Some expositors believe that this modification process will take place through God's release and utilization of atomic energy.

The term "RHOIZEDON" (RHOIZOS) is employed to describe "the great noise used in the destruction process." The great noise means "with a hissing and a crackling sound." It is interesting to note that. when the atomic bomb was tested in the Nevada desert, reporters stated that the explosion gave forth "a whirring sound or a crackling sound."

The term Peter employed was also used with commonality to describe the whirring of a bird's wings.

The term "melt," as in the elements shall melt with fervent heat, is etymologically connected to the word "thaw." This term "melt" means "to disintegrate, to be dissolved and carries the idea of something being broken down into its essential elements.

In II Peter 3:7, Peter describes the same destruction of the heavens and earth. He states, But the heavens and the earth, which are now kept in store by the same word, reserved unto fire.

The phrase "reserved unto fire" may mean "stored with fire," which is modernistically familiar, for atomic science reveals that the elements of the world are "stored with power." For God to bring about such a process will not be difficult since it has been discovered that there is enough atomic energy in a glass of water to run a huge ocean liner.

After the renovation of the earth and the atmospheric Heaven through an incinerating process, John in Revelation 21:2 states, "and I saw the holy city, new Jerusalem, coming down from God out of Heaven, prepared as a bride adorned for her husband."

The new Jerusalem is a city in which there is "no more sea." This possibly may refer to the removal or absence of the Mediterranean, or the oceanic makeup for presently 70-75 percent of the world is water: Obviously, all water will not be removed since Revelation 22:1, declares that "a pure river of water of life," clear as crystal proceeding out of the throne of God and of the Lamb, will exist in the New Jerusalem."

Revelation 21:4 reveals that "God shall wipe away all tears, remove death, sorrow, crying and pain, for the former things are passed away."

In the eternal city, "New Jerusalem," God declares that He shall "make all things new."

John describes the city in Revelation 21:16, "And the city lieth foursquare, and the length is as large as the breadth: and he measured the city with the reed, twelve thousand furlongs. The length and the breadth and the height of it are equal." The 12,000 furlongs dimensions of the New Jerusalem are equal to 1,500 miles in all directions. It could reach a city of such vast mileage from Maine to Florida and from the Atlantic Seaboard 600 miles to the west of the Mississippi, or an area occupying more than half of the United States. An Australian engineer calculated that the city would be 2,250,000 square miles, a size astoundingly evident compared to the city of London, which is 671 square miles. Listen, the New Jerusalem will be capacious enough to contain some 100 billion inhabitants if they meet the Salvation expectations of God!

Revelation 21:17 documents the equally awesome dimensions of the walls of the New Jerusalem. The passage reveals that city walls are 144 cubits high, which translates into 216 feet high.

The walls of the city are made of "jasper" (Rev.21:18) which is a transparent crystal, but the city itself is made of pure gold. Revelation 21:21 also states that the streets of the city were pure gold, like unto transparent glass.

A golden city or a street of gold seems utterly impossible until man's incredulity is squelched with the realization that the city of Smyrna, one of the seven cities of the Churches of Asia, in John's Revelation Church analysis, was noted for having, "the Street of Gold." If such an architectural manufacture was possible in ancient Smyrna, it is certainly within God's manufacture in the New Jerusalem.

It is a city with healing available for the nations (Rev.22:2) through the fruit produced from the restoration of the "tree of Life."

- No more curse. (Rev. 22:3)
- No more need for the sun. (Rev. 21:23)
- No more death. (Rev. 21:4)
- No more crying, tears, or pain. (Rev.21.4)

It is therefore clearly defined and accurately revealed why. Abraham "looked for a city" which had foundations whose builder and maker is God